This Is My Doctor

Adam Bellamy

Enslow Publishing
101 W. 23rd Street
Suite 240
New York, NY 10011
USA
enslow.com

Published in 2017 by Enslow Publishing, LLC.
101 W. 23rd Street, Suite 240, New York, NY 10011

Copyright © 2017 by Enslow Publishing, LLC.

All rights reserved.

No part of this book may be reproduced by any means without the written permission of the publisher.

Library of Congress Cataloguing-in-Publication Data

Names: Bellamy, Adam, author.
Title: This is my doctor / Adam Bellamy.
Description: New York, NY : Enslow Publishing, LLC, [2017] | Series: All about my world | Audience: Ages 5 up. | Audience: Pre-school, excluding K. | Includes bibliographical references and index.
Identifiers: LCCN 2016022716| ISBN 9780766081000 (library bound) | ISBN 9780766080980 (pbk.) | ISBN 9780766080997 (6-pack)
Subjects: LCSH: Physicians—Juvenile literature.
Classification: LCC R690 .B377 2017 | DDC 610.69/5—dc23
LC record available at https://lccn.loc.gov/2016022716

Printed in China

To Our Readers: We have done our best to make sure all websites in this book were active and appropriate when we went to press. However, the author and the publisher have no control over and assume no liability for the material available on those websites or on any websites they may link to. Any comments or suggestions can be sent by e-mail to customerservice@enslow.com.

Photo Credits: Cover, p. 1 Photographee.eu/Shutterstock.com; peiyang/Shutterstock.com (globe icon on spine); pp. 3 (left), 14 wavebreakmedia/Shutterstock.com; pp. 3 (center), 18 ERproductions Ltd/Blend Images/Getty Images; pp. 3 (right), 10 Steve Hix/Fuse/Corbis/Getty Images; pp. 4–5 Vereshchagin Dmitry/Shutterstock.com; p. 6 © iStockphoto.com/shironosov; p. 8 Hero Images/Getty Images; p. 12 Tom Wang/Shutterstock.com; p. 16. Alistair Berg/DigitalVision/Getty Images; p. 20 espies/Shutterstock.com; p. 22 Morsa Images/DigitalVision/Getty Images.

Contents

Words to Know 3

My Doctor's Office 5

Read More 24

Websites 24

Index 24

Words to Know

exam room

medicine

nurse

3

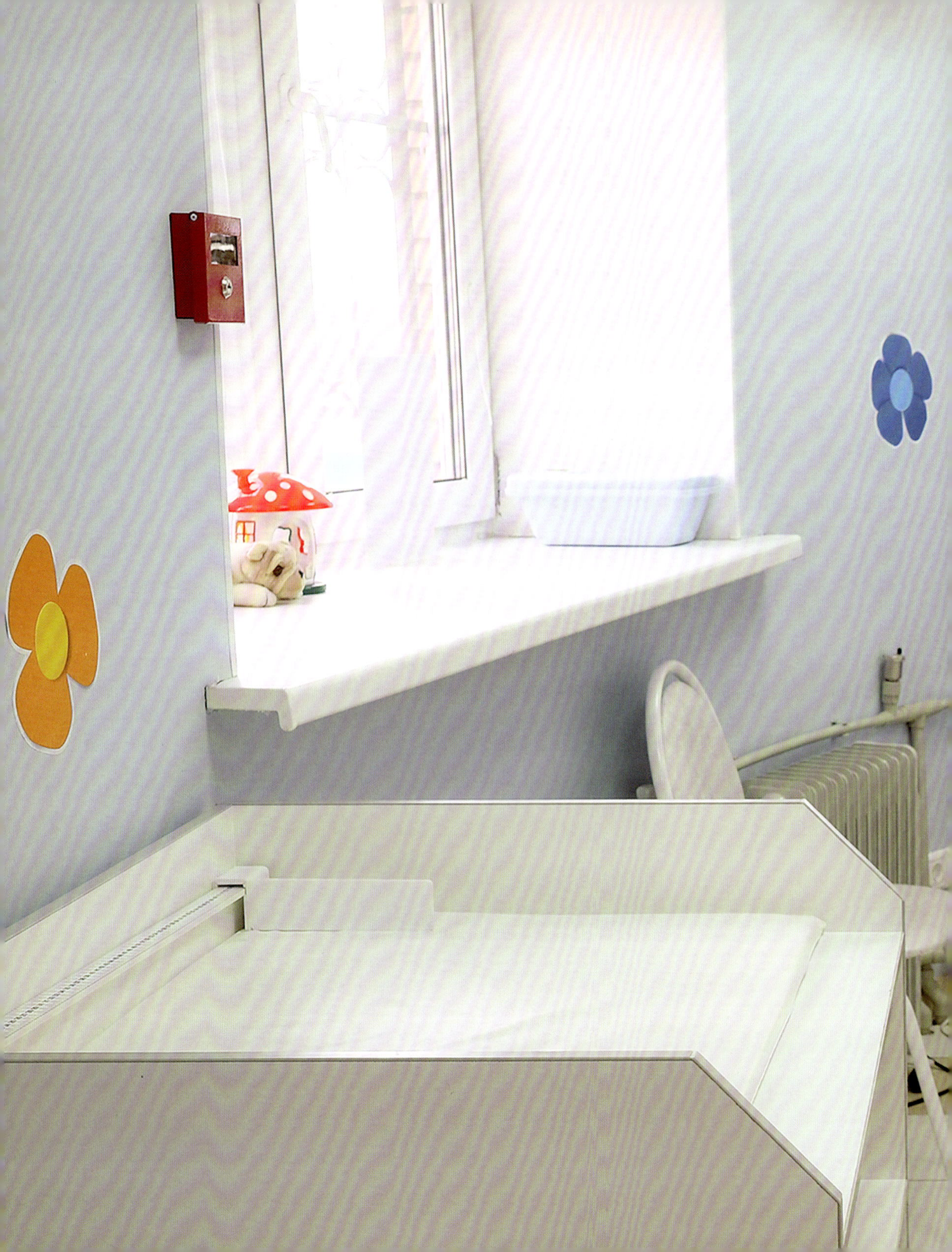

This is my doctor's office.

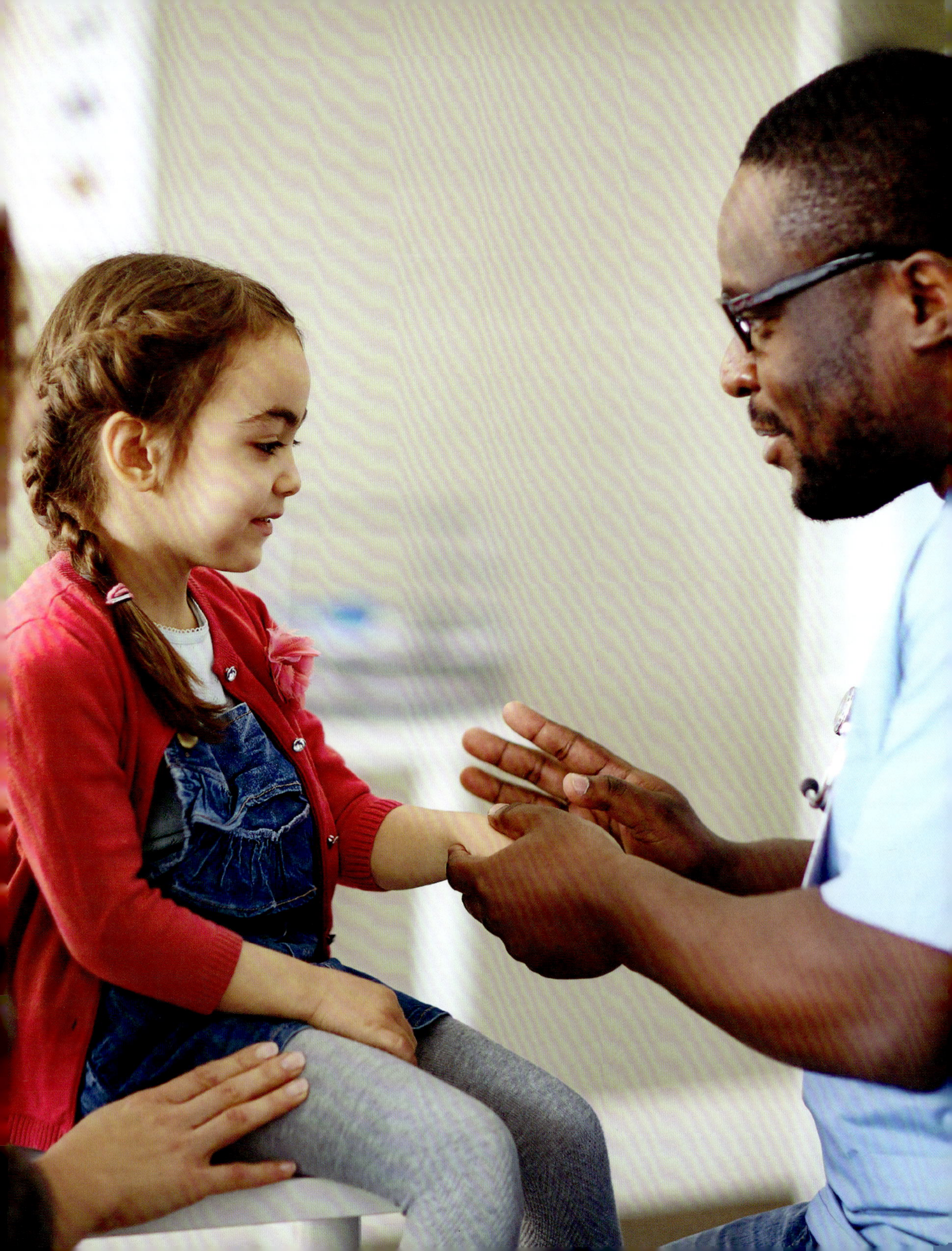

Every year, I go to the doctor to make sure I am healthy. This is called a checkup.

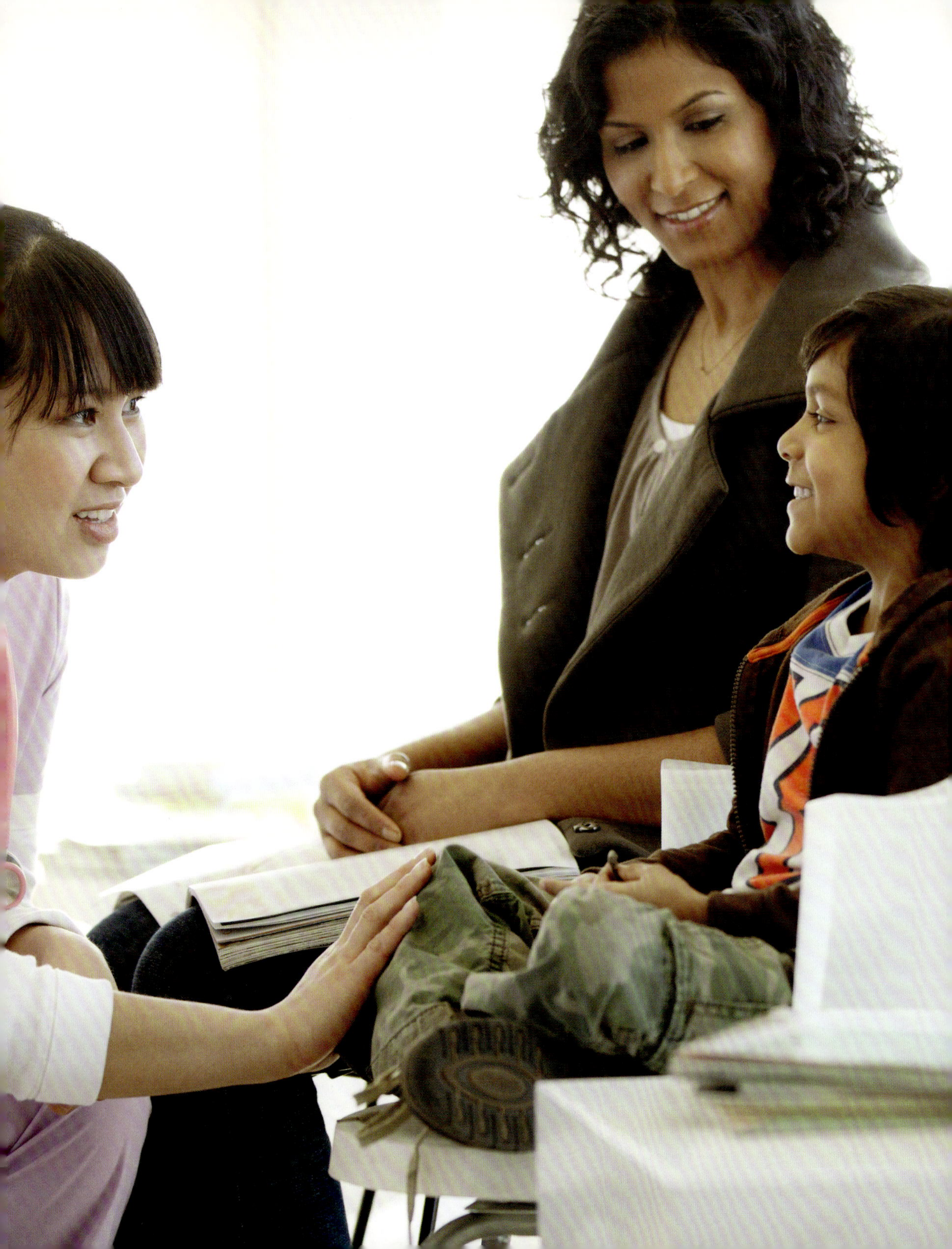

I sit in the waiting room until my name is called.

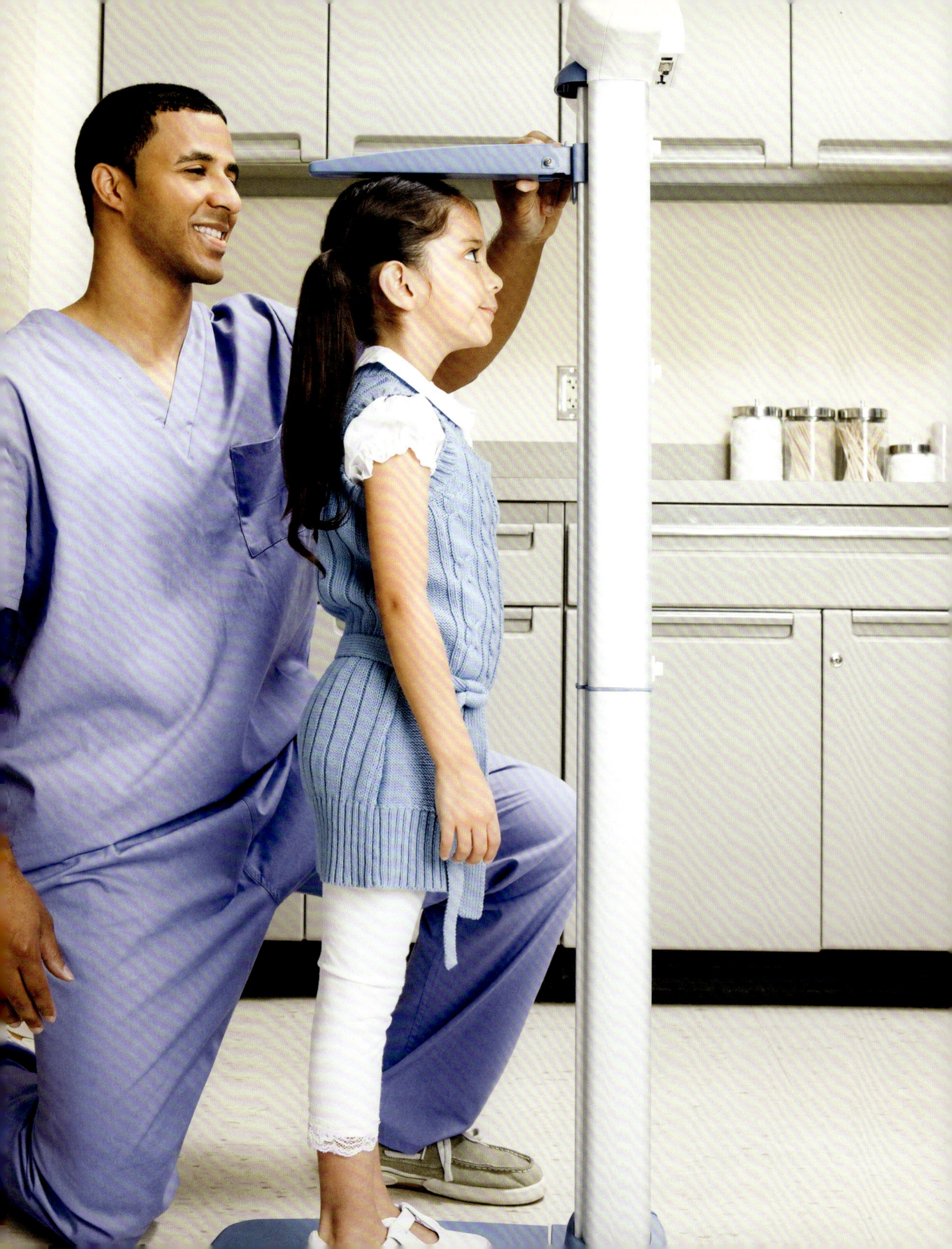

The nurse takes me to an exam room. He writes down how tall I am and how much I weigh.

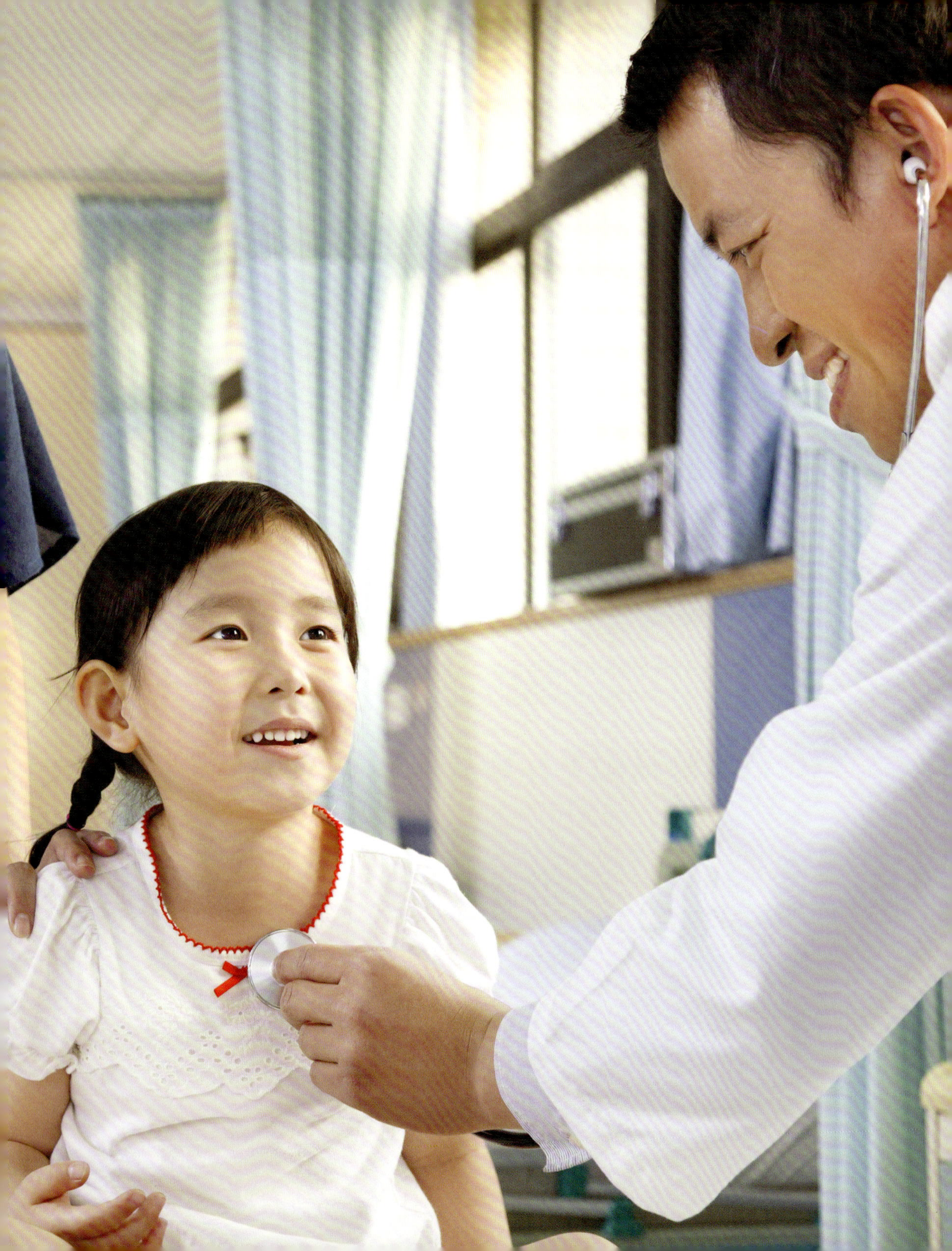

Then my doctor comes in. He listens to my heart and lungs.

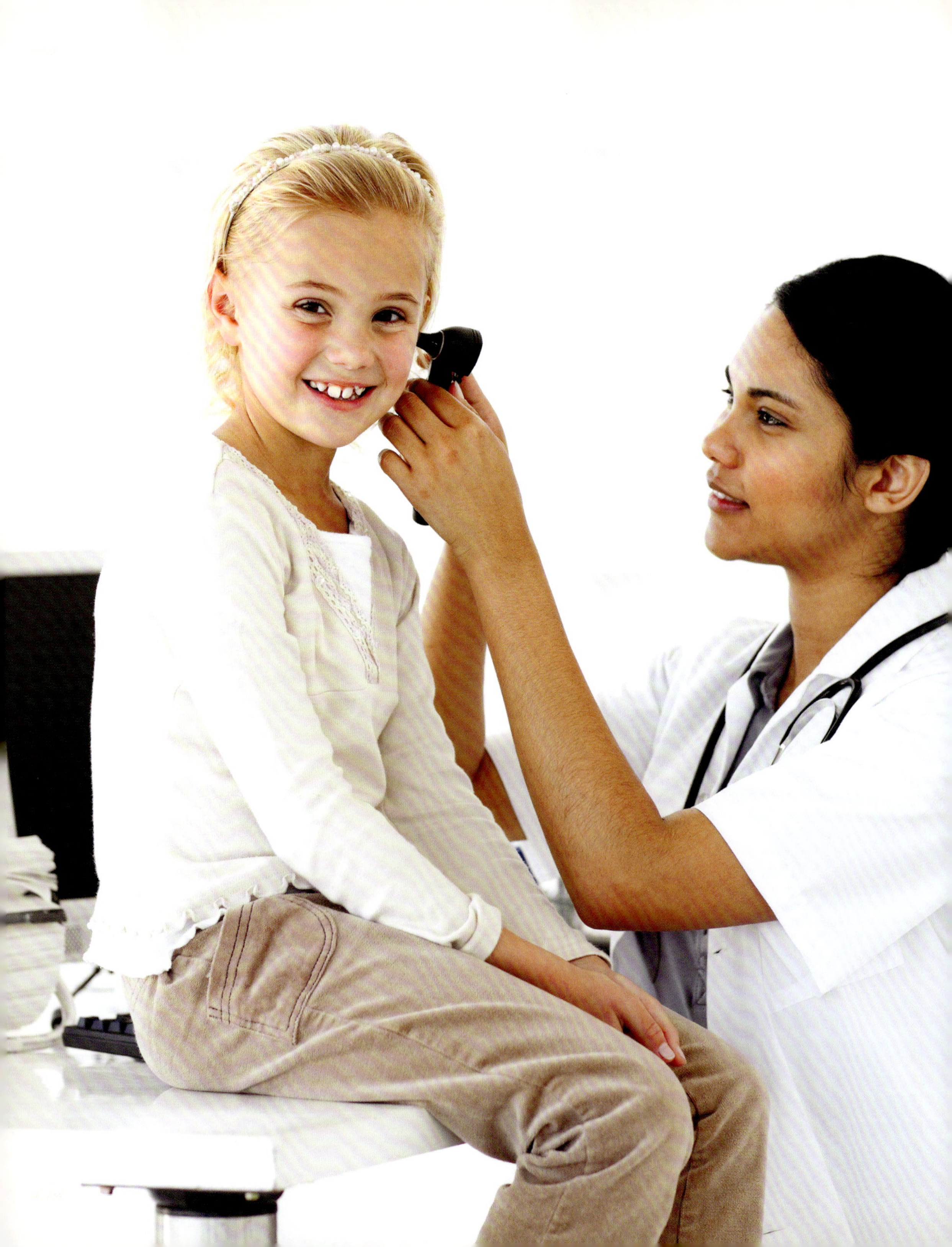

The doctor uses a small light to check my eyes, ears, nose, and mouth.

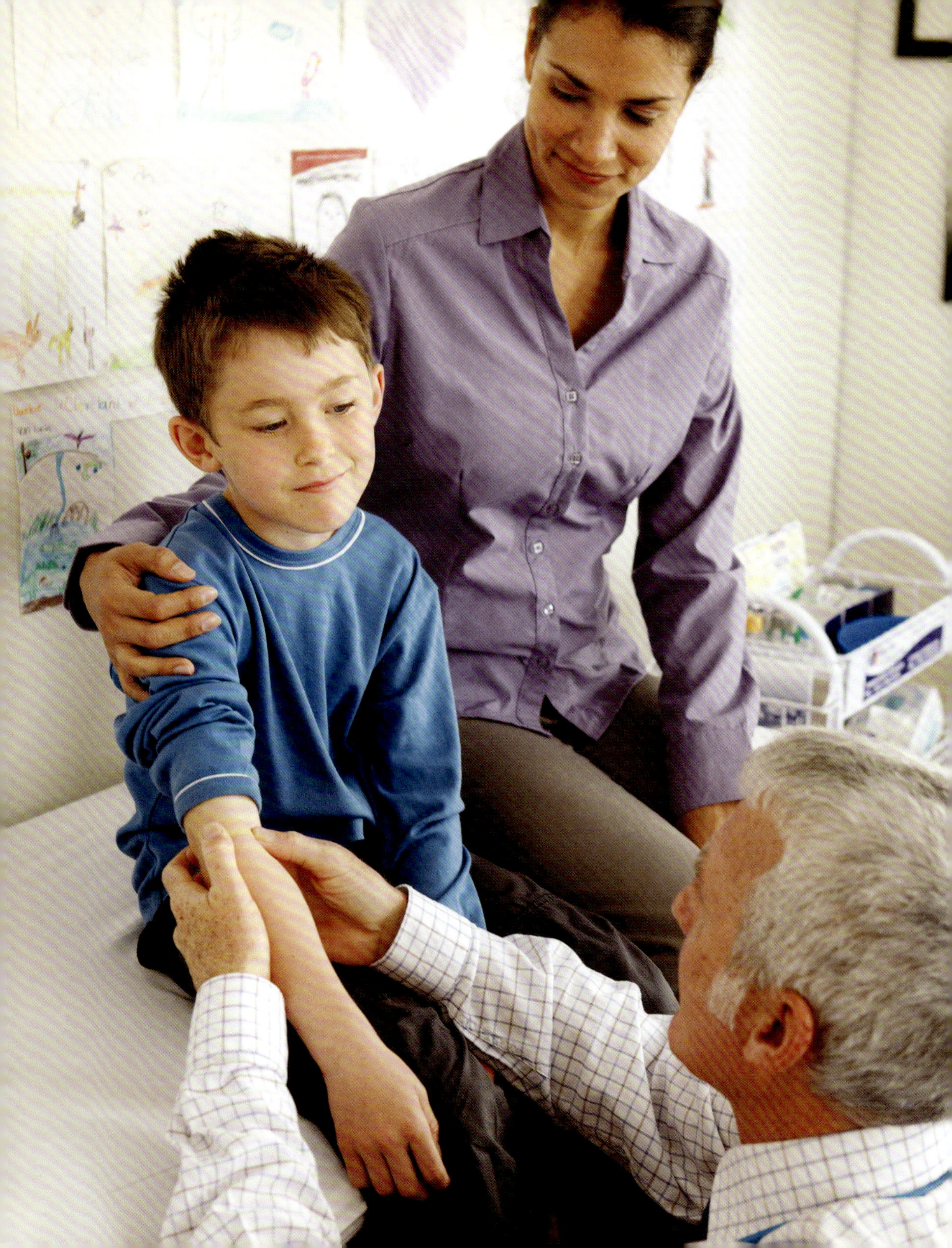

The doctor asks me questions about how I feel. If I feel healthy, my doctor does not have to do anything.

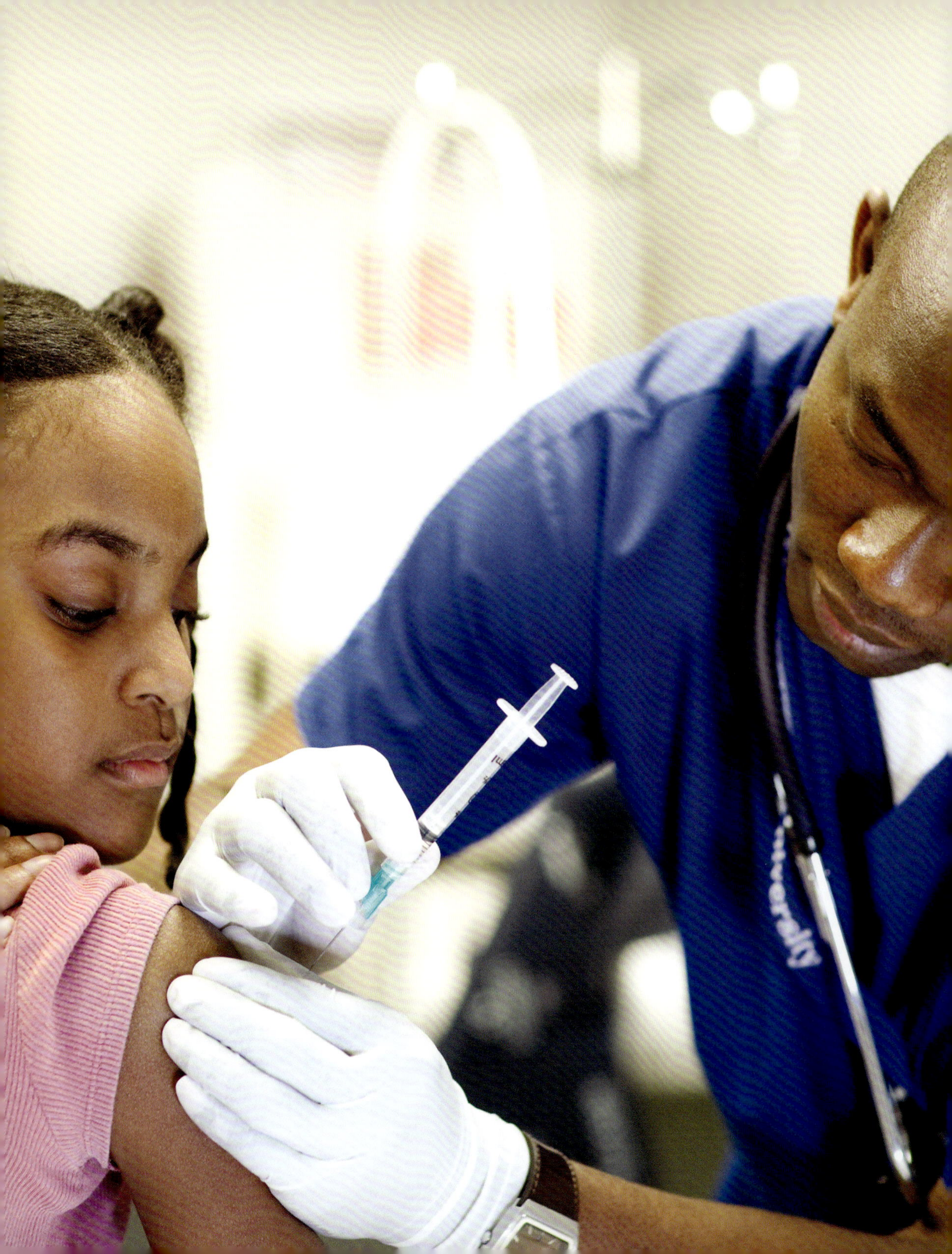

If I feel sick, my doctor will give me a shot or medicine to get better.

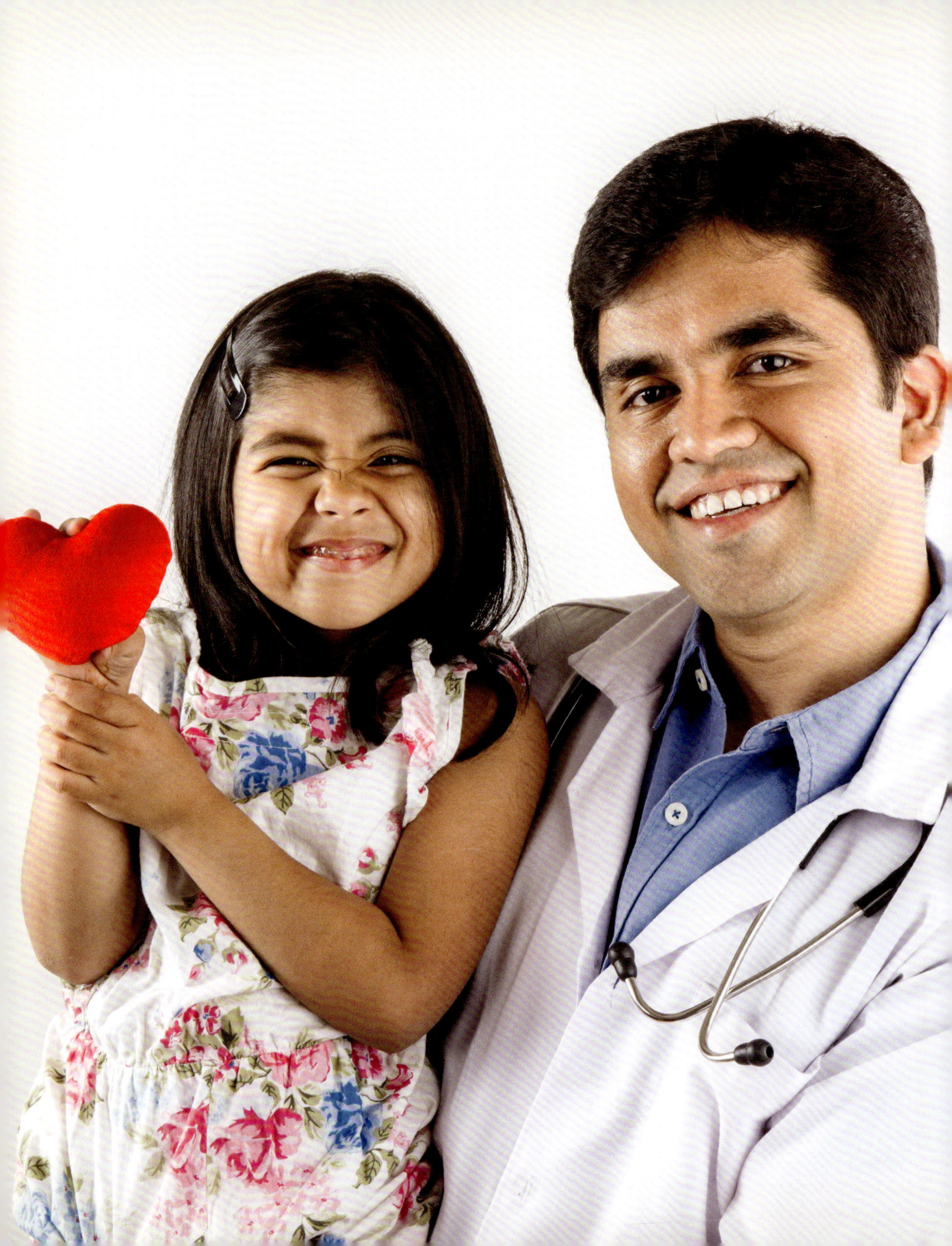

If I am good, I get a little surprise, like a toy, lollipop, or a sticker.

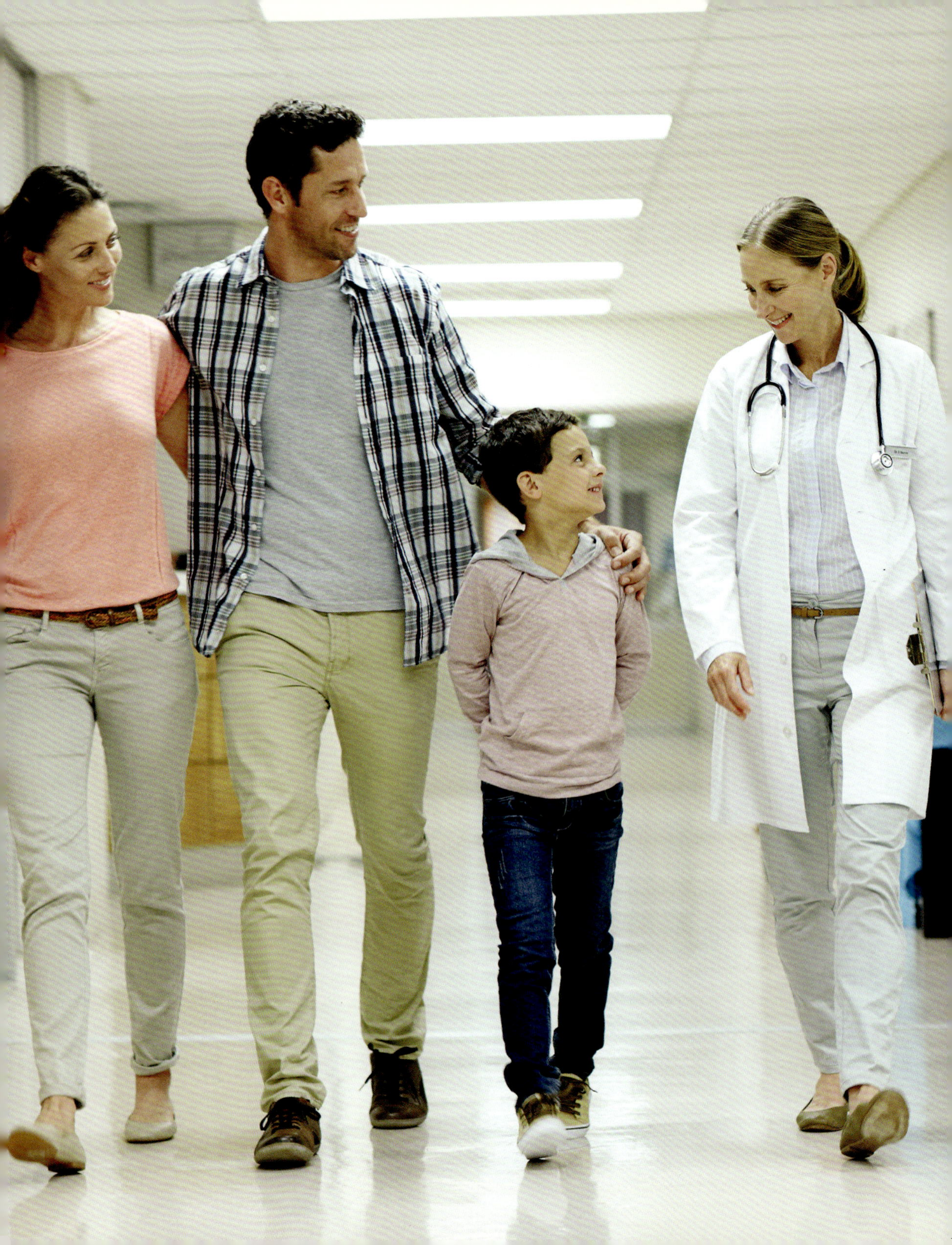

I am glad my doctor helps me stay healthy!

Read More

Marsico, Katie. *Visit the Doctor!* North Mankato, MN: Cherry Lake Publishing, 2015.

Phillips, Hannah. *Here to Help: Doctor*. London, UK: Franklin Watts, 2016.

Scotton, Rob. *Splat the Cat Goes to the Doctor*. New York, NY: HarperCollins, 2014.

Websites

KidsHealth
kidshealth.org/en/kids/going-to-dr.html
Learn more about a trip to the doctor.

PBS Kids
pbskids.org/sesame/games/elmo-goes-doctor/
Watch Elmo's first trip to the doctor.

Sesame Street
www.sesamestreet.org/parents/topicsandactivities/topics/doctorvisit
Watch a video about going to the doctor.

Index

checkup, 7
exam room, 11
healthy, 7, 17, 23
medicine, 19
nurse, 11
surprise, 21
waiting room, 9

Guided Reading Level: B
Guided Reading Leveling System is based on the guidelines recommended by Fountas and Pinnell.

Word Count: 142